STRING FIGURES

AROUND THE WORLD II

by
Sorena DeWitt

illustrated by
Robin Michel

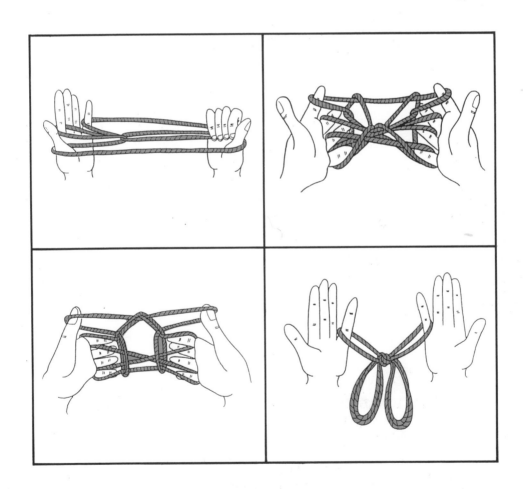

HEIAN

String Figures from Around the World II

Text by Sorena DeWitt
Illustration by Robin Michel

ISBN: 0-89346-827-4

First Printing 1995

HEIAN INTERNATIONAL, INC.
1815 W. 205th ST. STE# 301
TORRANCE, CA 90501

Printed in Hong Kong

TABLE OF CONTENTS

STRING FIGURES
FROM AROUND THE WORLD, VOL. II

Introduction

This is the second volume in a series of books about string figures and how to create them. If you enjoyed the first volume, then you are ready for the figures in this book. They are somewhat more advanced but just as much fun.

These string figures originate from around the world, and each one gives an insight into the people who created them. They used fishing line, leather strips, sinew, or hair that was finely braided. It is a very old art form that has been preserved by anthropologists when they studied these ancient cultures.

Making string figures is fun to do; the more you practice, the easier it becomes. Each figure has a name; several are like magic tricks, and some tell a story. As you perfect the easier examples, you will want to attempt the more difficult figures.

INSTRUCTIONS

Making the String

The first step in making string figures is creating the string itself. Any kind of string can be used, including cording or yarn. It needs to be two yards long-- one yard long when folded in half and the two ends are knotted together to form a circle.

The best knot to use is the square knot which is shown here:

1. Make the first part of the knot by laying the left end of the string over the right end, then tuck the left end under the right string. Pull the ends out far enough to lay the new right string over the left string.

2. Tuck the right string under the left string.

3. Tighten the knot to make it as small and as smooth as possible.

String Play Language

In order to follow the directions for each string figure, you need to know the special terms used for parts of your hand, parts of the string, and moves you make with each. The following picture illustrates the hand and string terms:

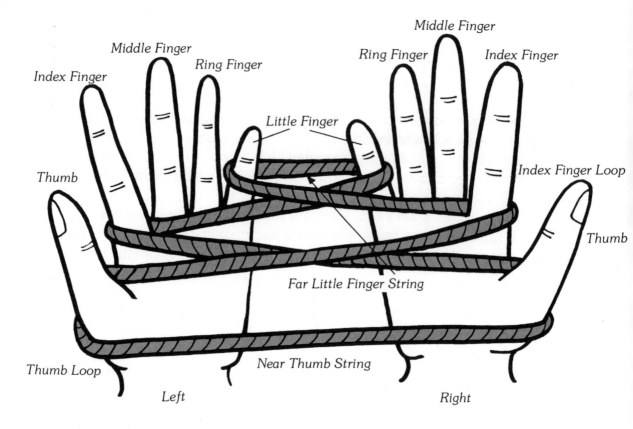

This picture illustrates the string referred to as the *palmar string*:

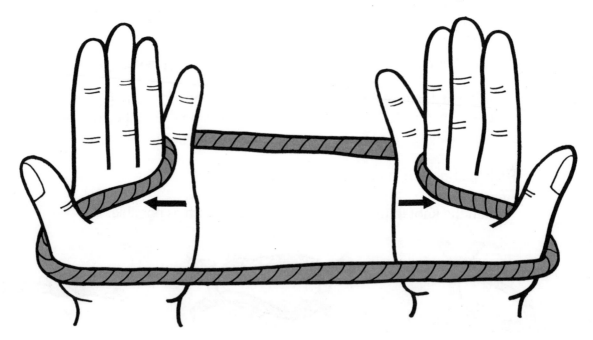

Many of the string figures begin with the same position or opening move. Following are illustrations of those most common in this book's string figures:

Basic Position

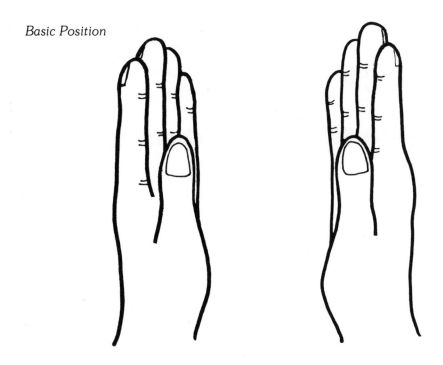

Position 1

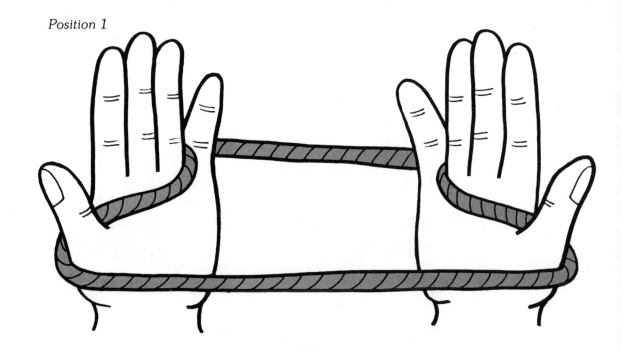

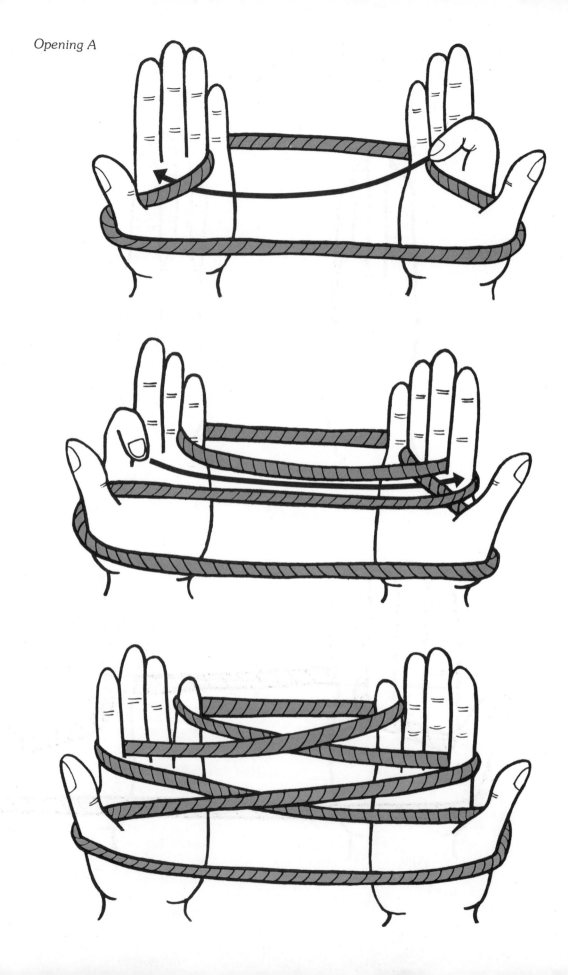

4

Navaho a Loop: This is a common move that you will use often when doing the string figures. It is done by slipping the lower thumb loops over the upper loops and over the thumbs.

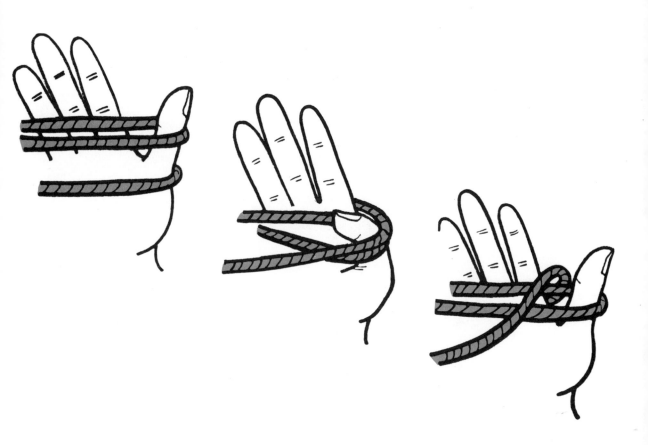

Share a Loop: This is done by pulling out the loop on one finger to also go over a second finger.

Extend: This is done by stretching your fingers out as far as they will go. This is usually done to show the finished figure.

Now that we have covered the basics, let's begin.

Throwing a Spear

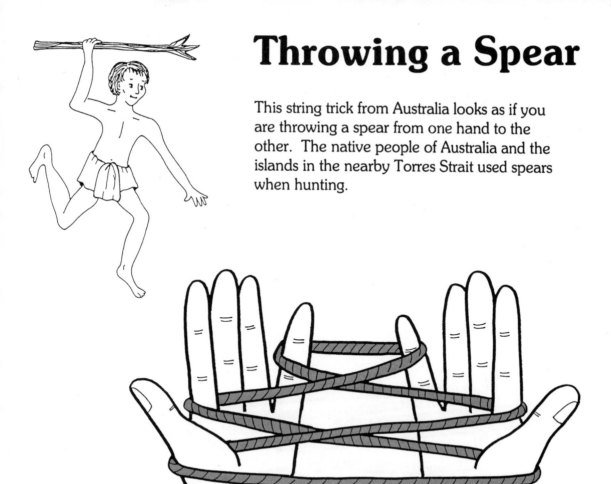

This string trick from Australia looks as if you are throwing a spear from one hand to the other. The native people of Australia and the islands in the nearby Torres Strait used spears when hunting.

1. Begin by making the "Opening A" figure; picking up the left palmar string with the right index finger first.

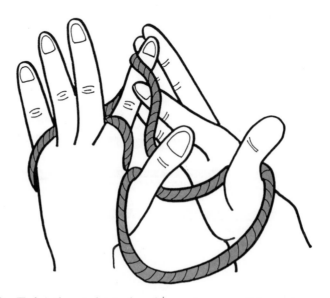

2. Take the right index finger loop and transfer it to the tip of the left index finger.

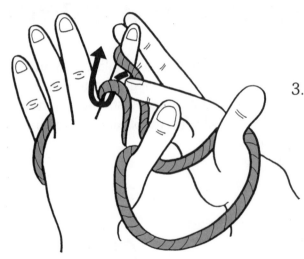

3. With your right index finger, pull the lower left loop up and over the left index finger so that it becomes the right index finger loop.

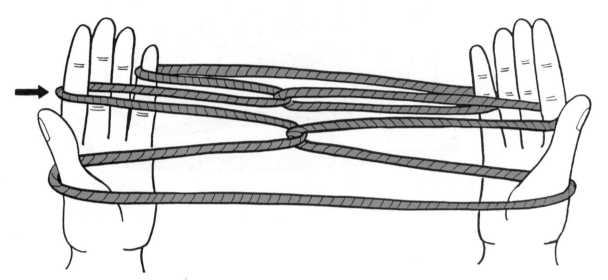

4. Pull your hands apart as far as you can. Drop the loop on your left index finger.

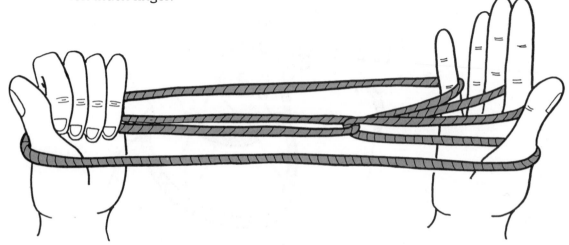

5. Pull your hands apart as you close your left fingers down into the left thumb loop. This will give you the spear with the three prongs on the right hand, and left fingers holding the handle on the left.

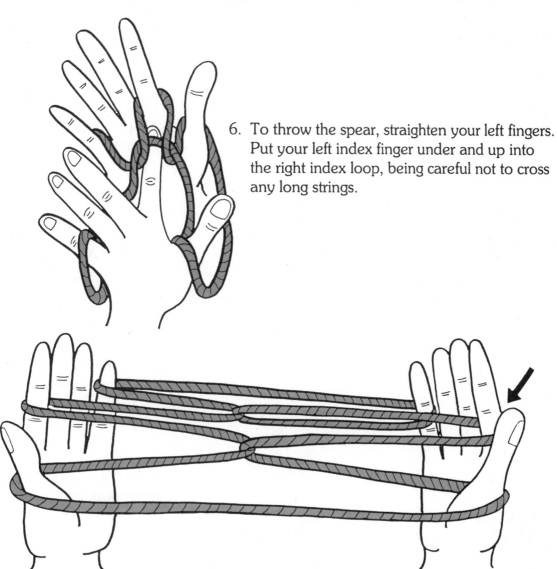

6. To throw the spear, straighten your left fingers. Put your left index finger under and up into the right index loop, being careful not to cross any long strings.

7. Pull your hands apart. Drop the right index finger loop.

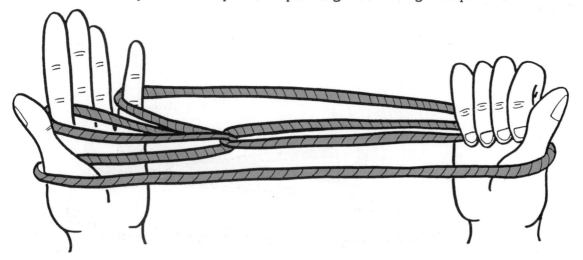

8. Pull your hands further apart and close your right fingers down into the right thumb loop to see the spear pointing in the other direction.

The trick of appearing to throw the spear from hand to hand can be repeated as many times as desired.

The Mosquito

This string figure can be a lot of fun, especially if you don't like mosquitoes. It comes from New Guinea in the Pacific Ocean.

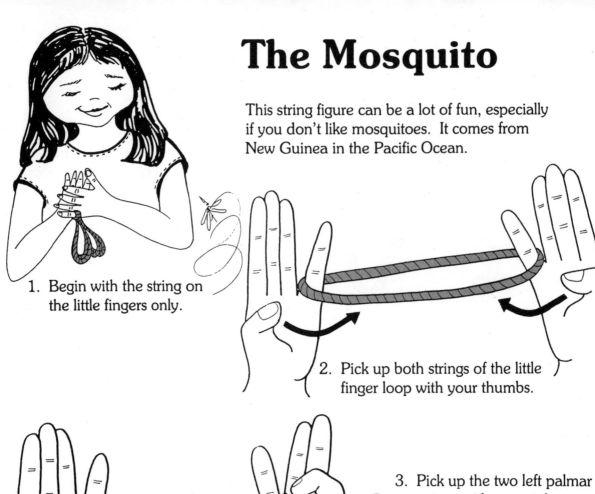

1. Begin with the string on the little fingers only.

2. Pick up both strings of the little finger loop with your thumbs.

3. Pick up the two left palmar strings with your right index finger.

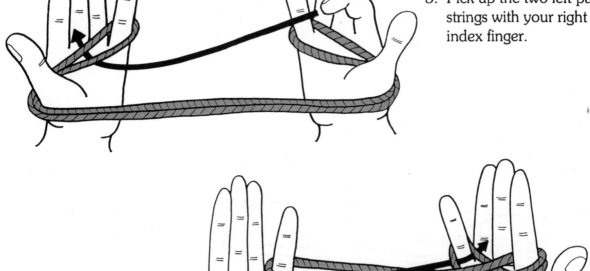

4. Use your left thumb to go over all the strings to pick up the two right palmar strings by the right little finger.

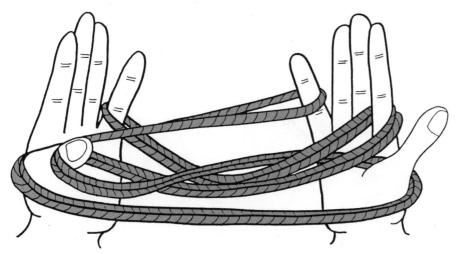

5. Navaho the loops on the left thumb.

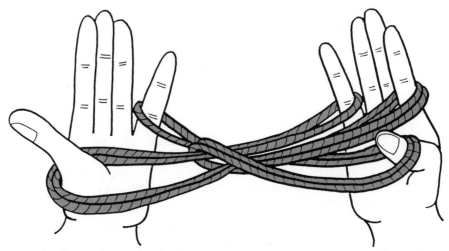

6. Drop the right thumb loops and pull the strings tight with your palms facing away from you.

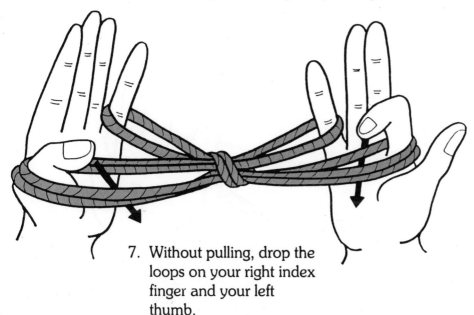

7. Without pulling, drop the loops on your right index finger and your left thumb.

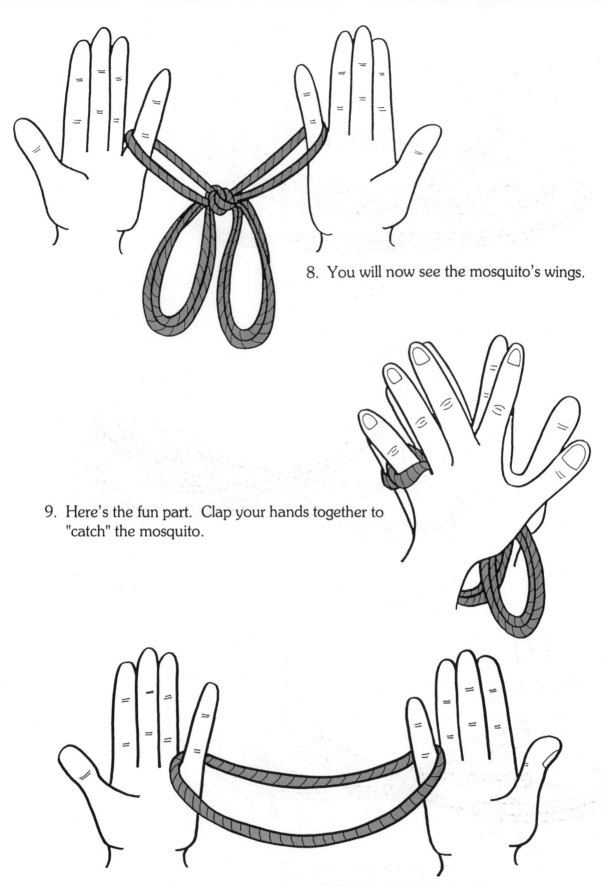

8. You will now see the mosquito's wings.

9. Here's the fun part. Clap your hands together to "catch" the mosquito.

10. Quickly pull your hands apart as far as you can and the mosquito will disappear.

12

Hogan

The Navajo Indians lived in hogans which look like this string figure. A hogan is made by packing layers of dirt over a heavy pole structure. This method creates a dome shape rather than a teepee shape.

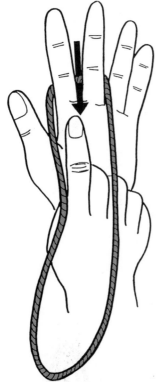

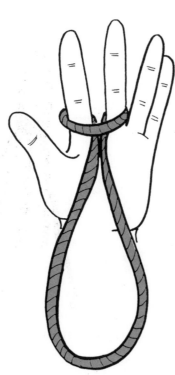

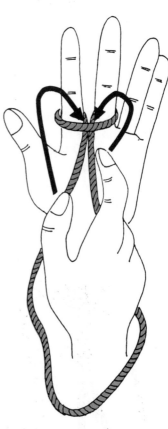

1. Drape the string around your left index and middle fingers as shown in drawing above. With your right index finger, go under the near string of the hanging loop, then in between the left index and middle fingers to pick up the back string.

2. Pull this string out under the front hanging loop to make a new hanging loop.

3. Using your right hand, go under the hanging loop, and up through the loop. Using your right index finger and thumb, go over the string around the left index and middle fingers. Pick up the two strings between the left index and middle fingers.

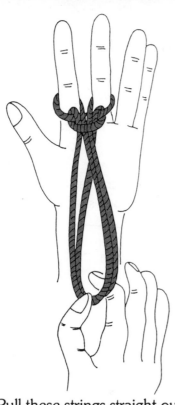

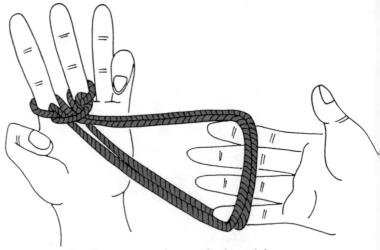

5. Put your other right hand fingers into these loops to make it wider, keeping the right index finger up and the right little finger down.

4. Pull these strings straight out and down through the hanging loop which is sliding toward your left fingers. Keep these two new large loops smooth and straight.

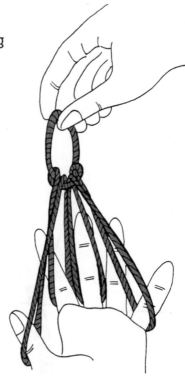

7. This makes the Hogan.

8. **BONUS**: While holding the loop with the right fingers, carefully remove the left hand fingers from their loops. You will see a hanging bunch of bananas.

6. The left little finger and thumb each pick up a bottom string. The right hand drops its strings. Then, gently pull the knot loop that is over the two strings hanging over the left palm.

Siberian House

This string figure comes from the Eskimos in Alaska; Eskimos are very good at this art form. This figure has two parts to it: the house, and the two people running away from each other.

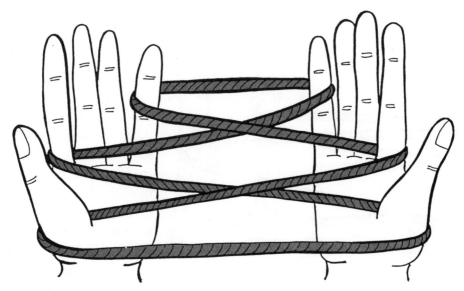

1. Start with "Opening A".

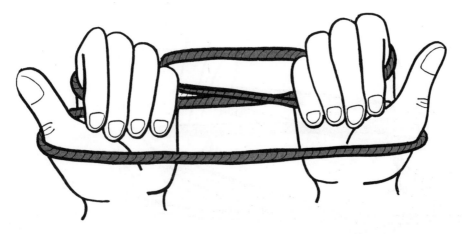

2. Turn your palms to face you, then put all your fingers down into the thumb loops. Slide the thumb loops over all the fingers onto the back of the hands.

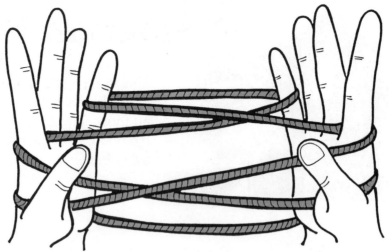

3. With palms facing each other, make sure the loops on the back of the hand are lower than the index loops.

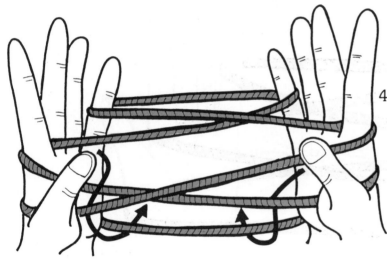

4. Take your thumbs and put them between the lower hand loops and the near index strings. Reaching under all the other strings, pick up the far string of the hand loop with the thumbs and bring it forward through the openings where the thumbs entered.

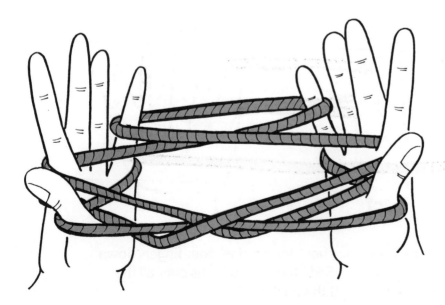

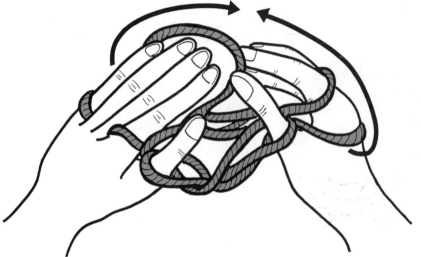

5. Carefully with the right hand, bring the back left hand loop up over the left fingers to the center of the figure. Do the same with the right hand back loop.

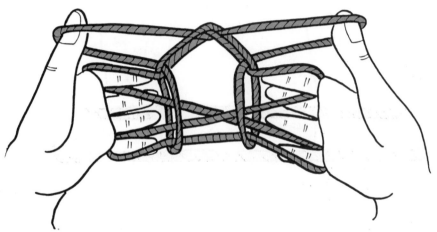

6. Extend your fingers with the thumbs up to see the Siberian House.

7. Drop the index finger loops and pull your hands apart gently. You will see two people running away from each other.

Japanese Butterfly

This is a very pretty string figure from Japan. It has some very unusual moves, so follow each step very carefully.

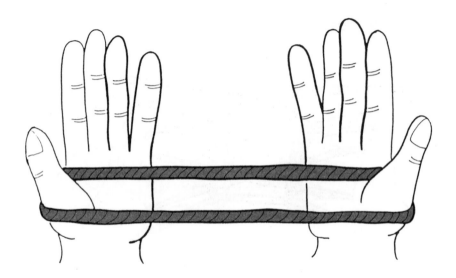

1. Put the string around your thumbs as shown.

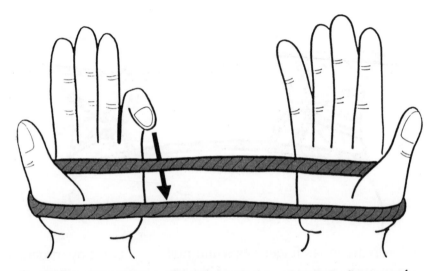

2. Pick up the far thumb string with your left little finger only.

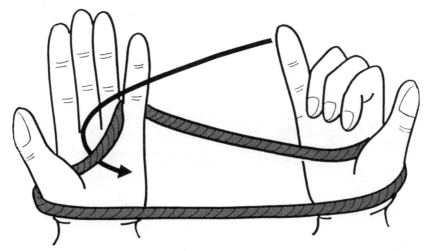

3. Bend all the right fingers down except the little finger. Put your right little finger down behind the left palmar string.
As you pull the palmar string, twist the little finger away from you, then up, and return to "Basic Position". Check to make sure the string looks as shown in drawing below.

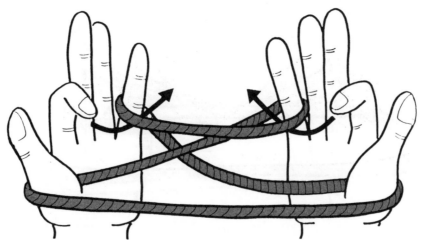

4. Pick up the near little finger string with your index fingers.

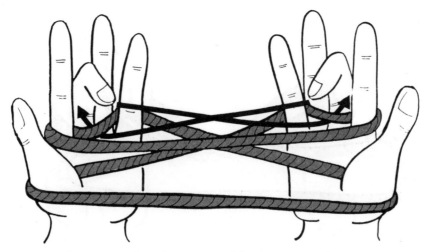

5. Do "Opening A" with your middle fingers and the short palmar strings in front of each middle and ring finger.

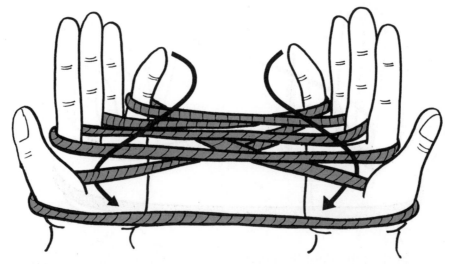

6. With your little fingers, pick up the far thumb strings and return to the "Basic Position".

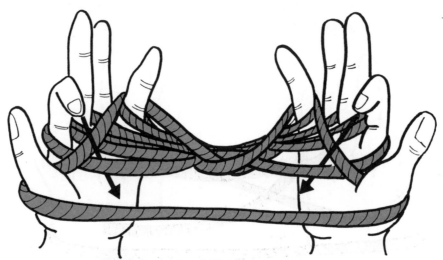

7. Put your index fingers down into the index loops over the palmar strings.

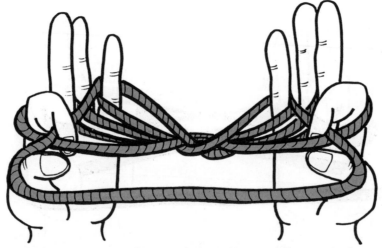

8. Holding tight to these palmar strings with your index fingers, drop your thumb loops.

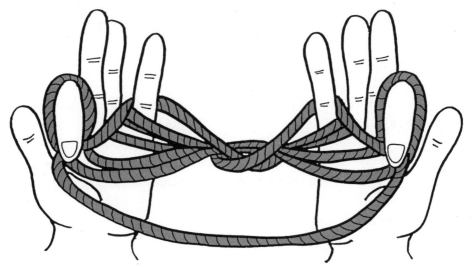

9. Face your palms toward you and let the old index loops slide off your index fingers.

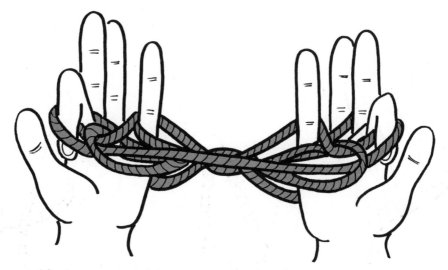

10. As you straighten your index fingers, the strings under them become the new index loops.

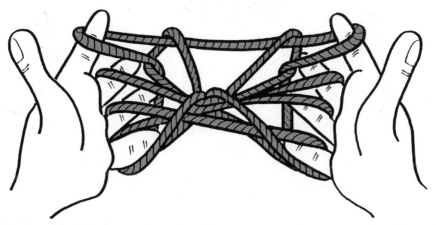

11. Face your palms toward each other again, and turn your hands so that the thumbs are up and the fingers are pointing away from you. You will see the Japanese Butterfly hiding in there.

Tallow Dips

This series of string figures is well known in Great Britain and Ireland. Tallow dips refer to the process of making candles. The wick is dipped into hot tallow many times until the candle is the desired thickness. Included is a story that accompanies these string figures.

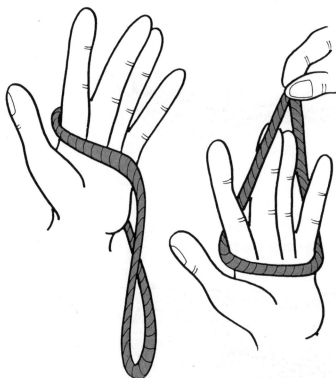

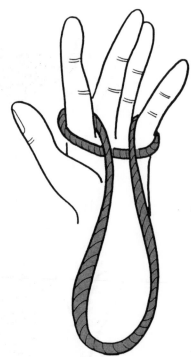

1. Lay the string across the left palm as shown, leaving out the thumb. Using the right index finger and thumb, pick up the two hanging strings behind the left hand.

2. Bring these strings up and over the left fingers, threading the one on the left between the left index and middle fingers, the one on the right between the left little and ring fingers. They should hang flat over the palmar string.

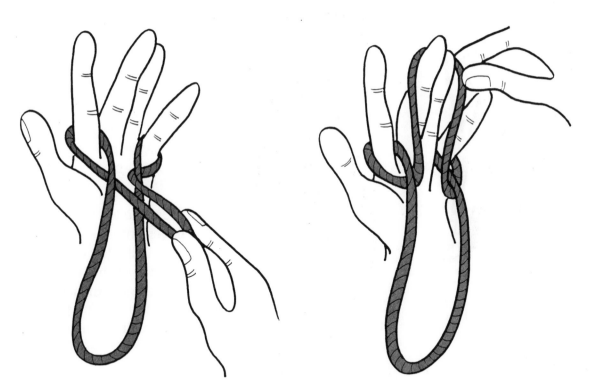

3. With the right index finger and thumb, pick up the left palmar
    string between the two hanging strings. Pull this string out far
    enough to make a loop that will fit over the left middle and
    ring fingers. There should still be a loop hanging down over
    the palm. Pull on this loop to tighten.

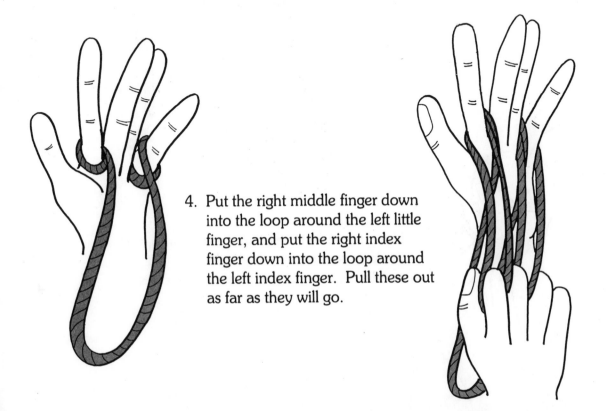

4. Put the right middle finger down
    into the loop around the left little
    finger, and put the right index
    finger down into the loop around
    the left index finger. Pull these out
    as far as they will go.

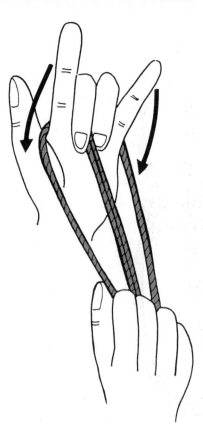

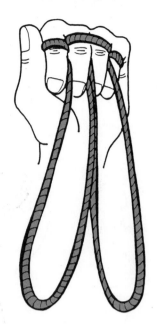

5. Close the left hand fingers into the palm putting the left index finger over the left near index string, the left middle finger into the left index loop, the left ring finger into the left little finger loop, and the left little finger over the left far little finger string.

6. Using your right thumb and index finger, take the two hanging loops and thread them through the loop over the back of the left middle and ring fingers. Pull them so they hang down the back of the left hand.

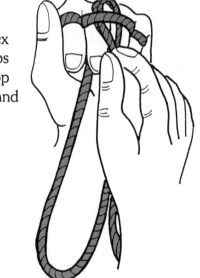

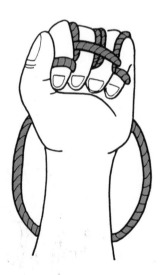

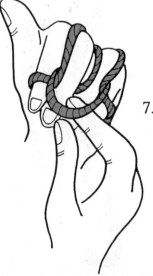

7. Using the right index finger and thumb, pull the loop that crosses the back of the left middle and ring fingers over the knuckles of these two fingers toward the palm.

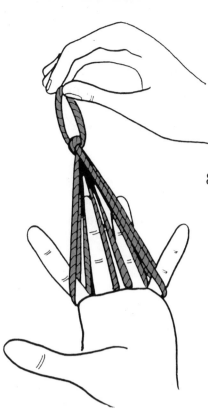

Story:

Once there was a man who stole a pound of tallow dips. He took them home and hung them on a peg.

8. Carefully and slowly pull this loop away from the left hand while opening the left fingers out. Holding the left hand palm up and pulling up with the right hand, you will see the four Tallow Dips.

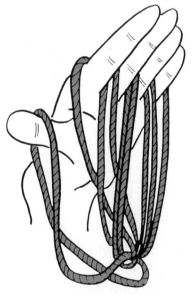

9. Put the loop held by the right index finger and thumb over the left thumb without twisting any strings.

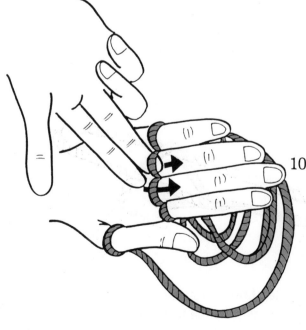

10. Hold the left hand with palm facing down and fingers pointing right. Using the right index finger and middle finger, hook the loops on the back of the left middle finger and ring finger. The back of the right hand's fingers should face the back of the left hand's fingers.

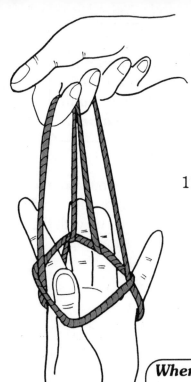

The man was very tired so he sat down on a chair and went to sleep.

11. With the right hand, pull these two loops up as far as possible. At the same time, turn the left palm upwards. This forms the chair the man sat on.

When the man woke up, it was dark. He got a pair of scissors to cut the tallow dips apart so he could light one.

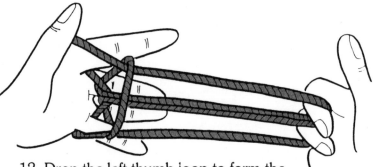

While the man was cutting off the tallow dip, a constable (an English policeman) came with his truncheon (an English policeman's club) and arrested him for stealing the tallow dips.

12. Drop the left thumb loop to form the scissors. Move right index and middle fingers up and down to show the scissors in a cutting motion.

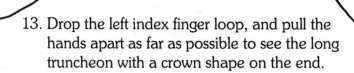

13. Drop the left index finger loop, and pull the hands apart as far as possible to see the long truncheon with a crown shape on the end.

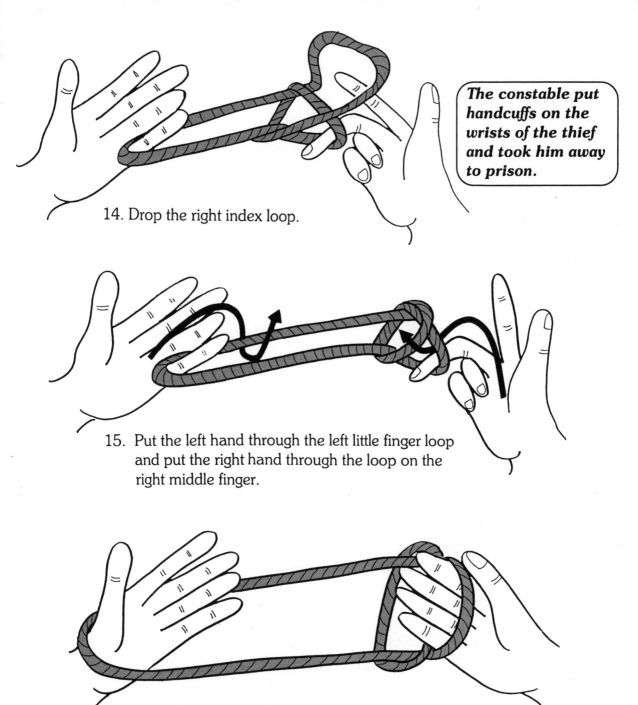

The constable put handcuffs on the wrists of the thief and took him away to prison.

14. Drop the right index loop.

15. Put the left hand through the left little finger loop and put the right hand through the loop on the right middle finger.

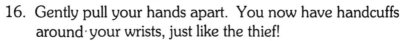

16. Gently pull your hands apart. You now have handcuffs around·your wrists, just like the thief!

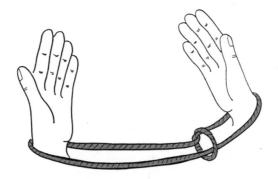

Resource List

Cat's Cradle, Owl's Eyes: A Book of String Games, Camilla Gryski, William Morrow & Co., New York.

Many Stars & More String Games, Camilla Cryski, William Morrow & Co., New York.

String Figures and How to Make Them, Caroline Furness Jayne, Dover Publications, Inc., New York.

Strings on Your Fingers, Harry & Elizabeth Helfman, William Morrow & Co., New York.

The American Indian, Oliver La Farge, Crown Publishers, New York.

About the Author:

SORENA DeWITT lives in Fremont, California, with her husband and five children. She has taught cultural refinement classes, served on many educational committees, and co-authored the children's almanac, *Guess What Day It Is.*

About the Illustrator:

ROBIN MICHEL has taught arts and crafts for children and is actively involved with art programs in various schools. She publishes a community news magazine and lives in Fremont, California with her husband and three children.